30-Days to Embracing Singleness

A devotional

Copyrights © 2015 Britt Dior. All rights reserved.

ISBN: 1519599129
ISBN-13: 978-1519599124

No part of this book may be reproduced, stored in a retrieval system, or transmitted by any means without the written permission of the author.

Printed in the United States of America. This book is printed on acid-free paper.

Cover designed by Genesis Dorsey of GigiCreates.

Because of the dynamic nature of the Internet, any web addresses or links contained in this book may have changed since publication and may no longer be valid.

Mommy, Daddy & Bianca

For just being there in a way that no one else could.

This book is for you.

What's Inside?

Week 1:
Day 1 – Acceptance
Day 2 – A Broken Heart
Day 3 – Loneliness
Day 4 – Green With Envy
Day 5 – Fear of the Future
Day 6 – The Dark Moments
Day 7 – Healing

Week 2:
Day 8 – Control Your Thoughts
Day 9 – Get to Know God
Day 10 – What Does God Want From You
Day 11 – Walking With the Promises of God
Day 12 – Everything is going to Work Out For Your Good
Day 13 – Chosen and Set Apart
Day 14 – How He Loves You

Week 3:
Day 15 – Finding Yourself
Day 16 – Happiness for Other People
Day 17 – Forgiveness is For You
Day 18 – Unplug
Day 19 – The Price We Pay to Settle
Day 20 – The Uncomfortable Places
Day 21 – Goodbye Past

Week 4:
Day 22 – Learning From Other People
Day 23 – Perspective
Day 24 – Tell Someone What You're Thinking
Day 25 – Dating
Day 26 – Don't Compromise Your Convictions
Day 27 – Male Friends
Day 28 – Sin Will Stop You

Week 5:
Day 29 – Your Journey is Unique
Day 30 – Rest, God Has Not Forgotten About You

Week 1

Week one is designed to tackle the bad stuff we feel when we're single. I wanted to focus on the feelings that nobody wants to really acknowledge because everyone is in such a hurry to get over rough feelings. The reality is that ignoring them doesn't make them disappear; it just makes them stronger when they decide to pop back up. It's so important to recognize the negative feelings as they come and actively work to turn them into positives. Week one isn't meant to make you feel depressed or experience pain; it's meant to encourage you. Although these feelings are natural you don't live in week one. You acknowledge it, learn from it, and then you move on.

Britt

Day 1 – Acceptance

I have learned to be content whatever the circumstance
Philippians 4:11

    As with anything, you can't move forward until you have truly accepted where you currently are. They say that once you have accepted "what is" you can then make changes to fix it if you don't like it. Well, being single doesn't exactly work that way. You can't just say "Okay God, I accept being single now you can move me to the next season of my life where I'm not single". God would probably get a good laugh out of a remark like that. Believe it or not that was exactly my thought process. Everyone kept telling me to stop focusing on wanting a relationship and just be content with my season and God would send my prince charming. So everyday I told God that I was happy being single and I actively waited for him to bring me The One. What nobody cared to tell me was that accepting this season was more than just talking the talk.

    When we truly accept something or someone we take it in the state that it comes in. Even if we desire for it to be more we take it as it is and we have peace about it. When it comes to being single that peace gives us the ability to acknowledge that this single season came from God and since only good things come from him then he must know what he is doing. Acceptance may not happen over night but if you are diligent in your prayers about accepting the season you are in then the peace will follow. The peace will also bring contentment, which is a state of peaceful happiness. Being happy while you are single doesn't mean that you won't be even happier with a spouse. It simply means you are making a choice to enjoy the situation you are in (as the scripture says) as opposed to being miserable every single day you are not where you want to be.

This whole journey of acceptance and contentment isn't necessarily something that happens over night. Some people become content a lot faster than others however once you become content you must practice *staying* content. Seasons are guaranteed to change and there will always be something you can choose to be unhappy about. Once you have truly developed a spirit of contentment you can shift your focus and begin to learn what God is trying to teach you in that season.

For you to pray: *Heavenly Father, I pray that you give me peace in this season of singleness. Reminding you every single day that I want a spouse is not going to change the fact that today I do not currently have one. I pray for the peace I need to embrace this season for everything you have designed for it to be. Teach me how to be content with where you have placed me, and the wisdom to acknowledge that you have not made a mistake nor have you forgotten about me. Remind me every time I forget that you know what you are doing in my life and I need only to trust you. You did not have to choose me to be single but you did. You saw something in me that needed to be developed and you are taking the time to do that before you bring the person you have for me into my life. Forgive me for not recognizing that you care that much about me. Jesus, I pray that during this time you do what you need to do in my life and mold me into the type of woman that can be used by you. In your name I pray, Amen.*

Day 2 – A Broken Heart

The Lord is close to the brokenhearted and saves those who are crushed in spirit.
Psalm 34:18

More times than not the initial onset of singleness is accompanied by a broken heart. Sometimes relationships end due to a mutual agreement that the people involved are better off apart and other times there can be a huge blow out. The pain that comes with heartbreak is no respecter of person. It doesn't care if you were betrayed and have a ton of reasons to be hurt or if you decided to randomly end a relationship. The separation, both physically and emotionally, of a person you have feelings for can cause a lot of pain and emotional turmoil.

I've been there more times than I have cared to. Sometimes it was due to my own fault when I kept the wrong relationships going and other times I was completely blind-sighted by another person's lies. Either way the pain was the same. I once cried for weeks over a very short relationship because my heart hurt so badly. During that time I went through all the emotions, including blaming God and giving him the silent treatment. Heartbreak made me a very angry and bitter young woman but it also taught me just how faithful God is. I had really persistent friends who were always praying for me and sending me scriptures. One day, I just gave in and softened my heart to let God in. That was when I realized he had never left me. He was just waiting for me to stop rejecting him so that he could heal my heart.

Maybe you have friends who are doing the same for you or maybe you don't. Regardless, I am here to tell you that God is indeed right there with you. He feels every single stroke of pain that you feel and he sees every tear that you cry. You might be upset with God and even mad at the world but he understands that too. However, don't stay mad at God because he is truly the only one that can put the pieces of your heart back together and he's so anxious to do so. I know it hurts to the point where breathing can seem hard but God is right there by your side paying very close attention to you. He's just waiting for you to let him take care of your broken heart.

For you to pray: *Dear God, Lord you are so amazing and faithful to me even when I am cold towards you. I thank you for not leaving my side but I also ask that you forgive me for pushing you away. Everyday is a struggle and sometimes the pain of my broken heart seems unbearable. I just need you to give me a new heart. I need you to come in and fix the pieces that are broken and make them whole again. I know there is a light at the end of this tunnel. There has to be but I just can't see it. Lord, my days are long and my nights are even longer. I don't know how long it's going to take for me to be whole again but give me patience as you heal me. I accept that I cannot heal myself, so God I willingly open the doors of my heart to let you in. I just want to be set free from this pain. In your Son's name I pray, Amen.*

Day 3 – Loneliness

God has said, "I will never leave you or let you be alone."
Hebrew 13:5

    Loneliness can be a very difficult thing to combat because it can stem from so many different places. Some people are lonely because they don't have anyone, or maybe they don't have the right person. They may know people and associate with different people but they don't have anyone that they can talk to. I've known people who have felt lonely because they simply didn't have anyone to hang out with. So they spent the majority of their time home alone or finding random things to do by themselves. My heart goes out to everyone who is experiencing some kind of loneliness but I always say an extra special prayer for the people who are surrounded by loved ones and still feel lonely.

    I was once that girl. I had let my singleness get me down so bad that I couldn't appreciate the good relationships that I had with my friends. There was a hole inside of me and I was convinced that a man would be the one to fix it because he would bring me completeness. What I didn't know was that humans can't fix that *kind* of loneliness. The feeling of completeness from a man or another person is just a façade, something that's not real. When we let other people fill us up we put ourselves in a dangerous place because those people take their "filling" with them if they leave. We must already have our loneliness issues fixed before we let a new person into our life. That way, if they don't stay we aren't left feeling lonely all over again.

    One of my harder lessons was letting God be the person to fill me up and make me not lonely again. We are taught that he is ALWAYS there and that he will NEVER leave us but that truth can be a tough pill to swallow because we cant physically see him.

However, we can feel him and, after all, loneliness is just another feeling. Loneliness is also a feeling brought on by Satan because he doesn't want us to live in the truth that God will never leave us. He wants us to be miserable and we can't give him that power. Nobody on this earth is promised to stay here forever but we are meant to survive the ones that leave us. Regardless of who leaves and who stays God is the one person who you can always count on to be there. As long as you walk with the knowledge that God is forever by your side then you don't give loneliness any place to exist. It will go away!

For you to pray: *God, I don't even have to tell you how I feel because you already know that my heart aches from being lonely. I just feel like I need somebody here with me. I've been so focused on the man that I want so bad and don't have that I didn't take time to realize I already had the Man of all men. I've had you with me this whole time. Lord, forgive me for pushing you to the backburner as if you were not enough. You are more than enough. Time and time again you have proven yourself faithful to me by not leaving my side. Your faithfulness sets the example. Lord, I know you're sending my mate... at the right time. So in the meantime, God, I pray that you can replace the loneliness that I have in my heart with your spirit. In Jesus name, Amen.*

Day 4 – Green With Envy

"Do not have a desire for your neighbor's house. Do not have a desire for his wife or his male servant, his female servant, or his bull or his donkey or anything that belongs to your neighbor."
Exodus 20:17

    Singleness can be a beautiful season if you have reached the point where you are absolutely content. However, when the desire to have a significant other consumes your every thought then you can develop a bitter spirit towards all the people that have what you want. Jealousy produces dissatisfaction and an unsatisfied person is an unhappy person.

    There was a time when I had been single for a while and it seemed like all of the people (women) close to me were getting into relationships and creating their happy ever after. One day one of them called me to tell me that her and her boyfriend were talking about getting married. They just knew they were the one for each other. She was so excited but I was so filled with envy that I couldn't rejoice with her. I didn't say anything but she knew I was uncomfortable so she changed the subject. I was so hurt that I couldn't be happy for her but I didn't know what else to do. I wanted someone to want to marry me so bad and it made me angry that it was happening for everyone else but me.

    Envy steals your ability to celebrate. It magnifies the "I want what they have" part of your brain and completely paralyzes the "I'm so happy for them" section. The bible clearly states that we should not desire anything that belongs to our neighbor. Anything! There is no need to. A huge lesson in being single is learning to trust God. When we trust that God will provide us with everything that he has for us, *at the right time,* there is no need to be jealous over what someone else has. What is for you is truly for you and God's promises do not return void. You do not have a significant other because it is not your season to have one yet. Trust God that he is coming and be happy for the people around you who are currently in that season. Rejoice in the blessings of others and God will bless you too.

For you to pray: *God please forgive me for harboring a spirit of envy and bitterness. Those are not of you and I am becoming unhappier as the days go by. Lord I want to be a good friend. I want to be able to celebrate the seasons that my friends are in. I want to be happy for them, truly happy. I want to be able to extend to them the kind of genuine joy that only you can provide. They deserve for me to be there for them and to be able to support them. I need you to come in and remove that poison from heart. Snuff that dark spot out with a light of gratefulness. I forget it sometimes but I am so blessed to be surrounded by people who are experiencing that kind of love. Because that kind of love is overflowing and will eventually fall on me too. So God, from this day on... I'm making it a conscious habit to be happy for other people because that's the best thing I can do as a friend. In your name Jesus, Amen.*

Day 5 – Fear of the Future

Don't worry about anything; instead, pray about everything. Tell God what you need, and thank him for all he has done.
Philippians 4:6

    Most types of worry are normally accompanied by fear and in life there are thousands of things that we can worry about. As a single person one of the main things you can worry about is being single forever. Especially when other people are floating around and living the life you want to live. It's so easy to fear that a romantic kind of relationship happiness will never happen for you. So many other anxieties are birthed from that type of fear as well and before you know it you are back at square one feeling sad and depressed because you don't see a happily ever after in your future.

    I've been there. I've faced what seems like some very tough times as a single because of fear. That's why I know that letting fear overtake you is a trap and a trick of the Devil. There was a time in my life where I cried everyday at the same time for 2 months in a row. Every day I would become overwhelmed and anxious and just cry. It took me a few weeks to figure out what was going on but when I did I felt crazy for letting it overtake me like that. The truth is that I was so afraid I would never be in a relationship that I started talking and going out with any guy that showed interest in me. I was signing up for internet dating sites, blind dates, and anything else that I thought would get me a man. It was driving me crazy.

    You have a choice when it comes to fear. You can choose to be worried like me and do everything in your power to make sure your happy ever after happens. Or you can choose to give your worry to God and just pray, be thankful, and pray some more. The best thing I could have done for myself was to stop worrying and start praying. If we truly give our worries to God then there is no need to fear the future. Trusting God means that you won't be afraid. It can be really easy or it can be extremely difficult. The choice is yours.

For you to pray: *Heavenly Father, I'm not exactly sure why I am doing all of this worrying about my future. I know that I have told you time and time again that I want to be happy in a relationship with the man of your choosing. Your word clearly says that the only thing I need to do is pray. God I ask that you remove that demon of worry from my life. Like Satan, it is following me around and whispering things like "you'll never be happy, no one will ever want you". Those are lies and I rebuke that spirit in your name. Lord, I trust you. I may have to remind myself of this often but I do God; I really do. Sometimes, I get carried away and let the fear that you don't see me get the best of me. Forgive me for insulting you like that. God I just pray that you increase my cup of faith so that it can completely remove any fear of the future that may be lingering in my spirit. Amen.*

Day 6 – The Dark Moments

Then Jesus said, "Come to me, all of you who are weary and carry heavy burdens, and I will give you rest.
Matthew 11:28

There is no season in our life that guarantees rainbows and sunshine all the time. Whether you have just recently become single or you've been single for a long time the journey will be tough at some point. There will be a time where you feel like all the light has left the room, even if it is just for a little while. Dark times look very different for each person. For some people it's just a moment of sadness and for others it may be a whole bout of depression.

My dark moments may have been some of the worst times of my life. At one point I was even diagnosed with bipolar depression which I refuse to believe is true. I spent almost an entire year seeing 3 different therapists, taking 2 different kinds of medicine, and practically being on watch for having suicidal thoughts. I wouldn't say that being single brought on my depression but my single status was definitely a trigger. Being single made me alone and being alone gave me plenty of time to think about all my past hurts and how unworthy of good love I must have been. Living had become overrated to me and I used to pray that God would just end my life. It was the darkest place I've ever been in my life but it doesn't have to be that way for everyone.

While you're single, Satan is going to try and use sadness as an opportunity to pull you down. He is going to do everything in his power to make you feel worthless and unlovable because his main goal is to destroy you. That is why it is important to fix your eyes on God at ALL times. Satan is a liar and anything that makes you feel bad is not from God. Yes, break-ups can make us sad but we do not set up camp in that sadness. There is no room for a pity party because Satan is going to be that guest the never leaves. So cry and cry some more if you need to, but let your foundation be in God. Let him be the source of your joy. That way, when the dark moments come you can pull on the strings of God and he will pull you out.

For you to pray: *Father God in the name of Jesus, I need you to come save me. Lord, I'm feeling my lowest right now and I need you to come and lift me up. My heart is so full of despair that it has made my entire soul miserable. Lord your word says for me to come to you if my burdens get heavy and they are too heavy to carry right now. I feel like I have the weight of a thousand broken bones on my shoulders and the pain that comes from that is just unbearable. I need rest God. My mind is at war and I know the thoughts I have are not from you but I don't know how to turn them around. I just need you to show me the light again. Shine a light through the cracks so that I know you are there. Lord, I need your healing to bring me out of this pit of darkness. In Jesus' name Amen.*

Day 7 – Healing

He heals those who have a broken heart. He heals their sorrows.
Psalm 147:3

Through his word God has made a lot of promises to us. One of my favorites is his promise to heal, especially the brokenhearted. Although having a broken heart isn't the only pain that comes from being single, a lot of that pain can grow from a broken place. At some point, every unmarried person that desires to get married is going to feel some type of sorrow. We go through it most when we have our moments of doubt where we feel like God has forgotten about us. Those are the places that God wants to heal. Healing is a part of the light that is at the end of the tunnel.

Healing is different for everyone and it definitely doesn't come in the form of an instant magic spell. My healing journey took a while. I carried the scars of almost 10 years worth of bad relationships. Like I've shared before, I had to go through a lot of counseling sessions just to begin to heal. Once I stopped blaming God I had to spend a lot of time in prayer and in the word to become healed. Even after a year of being on my healing journey, I still was not 100% healed. But I was also not the same broken person that I once was. At some point you will be 100% healed and feel like a brand new person but you may also carry a scar or two that reminds you of your brokenness and God's mighty power.

Healing also isn't something that's going to happen overnight. If you're on your healing journey now then keep going. If you haven't started it, now is the perfect time to let God in. God has clearly stated in his word that he heals the broken hearted and every single sorrow they have. So if you're hurting do not fret.

Have patience because the healing is coming. More than anything God wants to give you a new heart, a heart that is full of hope and believes in His promises. A heart that will be strong enough to survive but soft enough to love again. Allowing God to heal you is the only way that you will be able to embrace your single season for the wonderful time it is meant to be.

My prayer for you: *Father God I pray for the person reading this. I pray with them as they pray for healing over their life during this time. This can be a tough season but I know that you have designed it to be a beautiful and purposeful time in their lives. You know the desires of their hearts and their cries have not reached deaf ears. Lord I pray that you do whatever it takes to bring healing to their hearts, their mind, their spirit, and their body. I pray that you put the right people in their lives to help them during this time, the kind of people who will pray for them and speak life over them. Jesus I pray that you make them over again, make them newer and better than before. The enemy thought he'd won when he saw them crying but Father I rebuke him away from your daughter in Jesus' name. He has no claim over her life and the pain he is trying to cause is going to return to him null and void. Father I pray that you heal the places that hurt the most first, the ones that cause the most tears. I lift your beloved daughter up to you. In Jesus' name, Amen.*

Week 2

This week is one of my favorites because it focuses on strengthening your relationship with God. God comes before everyone and everything else and from him ALL blessings flow. It's so important to utilize the single season for what the Apostle Paul says it is to be used for: to focus on God and completing His will. So many saved and unsaved people are aimlessly wondering about with no sense of purpose because they don't know God. Really know God, the kind of knowing that only happens when you carve out time and sit before him. This week's main goal is to help draw your focus back to him. I know from experience how difficult that can be when your heart is trying to heal. I pray these next 7 days help you find your way back to God.

Britt

Day 8 – Control Your Thoughts

We break down every thought and proud thing that puts itself up against the wisdom of God. We take hold of every thought and make it obey Christ.
2 Corinthians 10:5

As with any season in our life it's important to be aware of our thoughts. In order to get the most out of each phase of life we must be conscious about where we are putting our focus and how that focus is benefiting our life. Being single can be tricky because from day to day our thoughts can go through past, present, future and bring a mix of emotions with it. It's imperative that we don't let that happen, especially as Christian women. We have to fix our eyes on God and begin by asking God why he has placed us in this season. Our thoughts will run our lives if we don't control them first. Sometimes it's as simple as saying, "hey, I'm not going to think about this!" and begin moving forward. Other times it takes a lot more effort.

In the past, I was guilty of letting my thoughts get away from me. That was part of the reason why I had to go to counseling for so long. I was constantly worried about what wasn't happening in my life and what I wanted to happen that I was completely overlooking the present state of my life. I eventually had to come to terms with the fact that I could not force God (or anyone else) to do anything that he wasn't ready to do. Since I was going to be single for as long as God wanted me to be then I might as well shift my focus to Him and think about the more positive aspects of being single. At least I could enjoy that season and be happier instead of complaining about not having a man.

One of my best friends, Arkia D., gave it to me straight one day. She told me that if I only focus on what I don't have then how can I truly appreciate what I have sitting right in front of me. Sometimes you have to dive head first into your current state in order to get your next blessing. We have to let God move in his time and not ours. Once we come to terms with that then God can answer the question of why we're currently single. God makes no mistakes so if he placed us in a certain season then it is for a purpose, and that purpose will be for our good. Trust me, take advantage of being single because the day will come when you are no longer single and you will yearn for the days where the only other grown-up you had to worry about was you.

For you to pray: *Lord, first of all I pray for forgiveness for focusing my attention on things that I can't control. I don't realize just how blessed I am to be in this season. Life is so good around me but I can't even enjoy it because I'm worried about the things that I don't have and the things that I want. Right now God, I'm going to open my mind up to you and shift my focus towards you. I want to be grateful during this time and for the blessings that you have already given me because I know that life could be much worse. Whatever it is you are trying to do in my life and mind, do it! I'm getting out of the way so that you can have your way in my life Lord. God I pray that this precious season is not wasted and you move in my life like never before. I just want to function in your will Lord and give you all my thoughts. In your name, Amen.*

Day 9 – Get to Know God

Seek the Kingdom of God above all else, and live righteously, and he will give you everything you need
Matthew 6:33

    Ask yourself who or what is most important to you right now. If your answer isn't God or at least your relationship with God then you may have to reevaluate some of your priorities. Some people don't seek out a relationship with God because they think it's going to be this overwhelming thing that will take up the majority of their time if it is done right. That's not the case at all. Our relationship with God is supposed to be just like our relationships with our closest friends. We have to get to know God the same way we get to know someone else so we have to spend time with him. Unless God called you to do this there is no need to spend 24/7 at the altar in an attempt to know God. Your relationship with Him will grow over time.

    I'm not sure why I thought I didn't have to work on my relationship with God. I just thought if I said halfway prayers to him in the morning and read a scripture here and there that it would grow. Once I got passed the stage of blaming God for of all my relationship problems I truly desired to have a real relationship with Him. I was just too lazy to actually do any real work for it. Getting to know God meant that I had to pick up my bible and read it. Not just read the words but actually study it to really understand what the scriptures meant and how I could apply it to my life. Texting my friends and surfing the Internet was just a little more entertaining. So I did that instead and my spiritual life did not grow. I didn't get serious about God until Satan was trying to attack my life and I couldn't fight back. I didn't know enough about God to know that Satan was a liar and God had promised the opposite for my life.

You don't have to wait until the Devil tries to attack you with his lies about your life. It's never too late. Getting to know God can start with taking the time to talk to him through prayer without distractions, even if it is for just five minutes. The next five minutes can be spent going over a few scriptures. Then everyday it can grow from there. Satan and his demons are never going to stop trying to attack you. They are always going to be somewhere in the background telling you how you'll be miserable and single forever. When you know God, truly know God, you know that nothing the Devil says is true. The bible is clear that if we fix our eyes on God then he will give us everything we need. Our main job is to seek God (daily) and let him take care of the rest.

For you to pray: *Dear God, I thank you for always being there and patiently waiting for me to come and seek you. I thank you for never turning your back on me even when I wasn't interested in knowing you. I want to get to know you more God. I want to have the kind of relationship with you that I have with my best friend, but an even closer one. You have been so good to me and I want to be able to say that I am a friend of yours. I want to be able to fight Satan back with your truth. Jesus, I want to know you more. Amen.*

Day 10 – What Does God Want From You

Now may the God of peace, who through the blood of the eternal covenant brought back from the dead our Lord Jesus, that great Shepherd of the sheep, (21) equip you with everything good for doing his will, and may he work in us what is pleasing to him, through Jesus Christ, to whom be glory for ever and ever. Amen
Hebrew 13:20-21

    The only person that can tell you what God wants from you during any time in your life is God. Through His word he has already told us that there is a season for everything and no season is in vain. God uses all of the seasons in our life for our good, including the single season that so many of us would rather not be in. That's why it's so important to get to know God so that he can tell you exactly what he wants from you and what he wants to do for you while you are single.

    Everyone's message from God is different. Some days I feel like I know exactly what God wants from me and other days I feel as though I'm way off track. However, I've come to terms with the fact that God wants to use me to do his will. I am but a pen and God is the writer. But why would God want to use somebody like me, someone with such a colorful past? I find the answer to that question every single time I talk to someone who is going through a storm that seems to be rooted in being single. I wouldn't have chosen this journey for myself but I count my blessings to be used by God to help someone else not go through the rough patches that I went through.

    Regardless of what God wants from any of us, the goal is always the same. God simply wants us to do HIS will but He has a different will for each of us. Sometimes we are afraid to do God's will because we think that what he wants doesn't include what we (think we) want. If that is the case, trust me, you are not losing out on anything. We have to trust that God ultimately knows what's best for us when we set out to do his will. If we are following God then he will give us the desires of our hearts. He will tell our hearts what to desire and then he will fulfill those desires. More times than not his desires for us are far greater than anything we could ever want for ourselves. He just wants us to do our part and allow Him to do His.

For you to pray: *Lord, you are amazing and I give you the highest praise. God I don't know what it is that you want from my life right now but I know that I want to do your will God. I want to be used by you Lord. Please show me the way. Use whatever and whoever you need to use to reveal your will to me. I want to live a life that is pleasing towards you, a life that is guided by your direction. I just need you to show me the way God. Amen.*

Day 11 – Walking With the Promises of God

I am with you and will watch over you wherever you go, and I will bring you back to this land. I will not leave you until I have done what I have promised you."
Genesis 28:15

    It is easier than you think to forget what God has promised you. Especially if you just *read* the word and you didn't actually *study* it. Being single is definitely a journey, as with most seasons in life. However, the things we learn in this season will help to build the foundation we will need in the seasons that follow. One of the key pieces of that foundation is remembering what God has promised you. I cannot stress the importance of letting God's word become a part of your natural make-up. I can only tell you that you will have really good days and you will have really bad days. Regardless of what the day brings if you are carrying God's word in your heart then you're already in a good position.

    I remember one day when I was praying my mind went to all of the situations that had caused me some type of strife in my life. It wasn't a bad day or anything I was simply just trying to have some quiet time with God. I didn't even pull my bible out. Just as quick as my mind (or the Devil) tried to remind me of my past the spirit instantly started reminding me of scriptures that I had read relating to the situation I was about to be upset about. I didn't even know I knew those scriptures by heart. But my heart remembered what I fed it at the time that I needed to be reminded of it most.

    This is not to say that every time you're in a rough situation you will automatically remember scriptures because you might not. This is, however, to encourage you and let you know that God's promises are always there. It is a good idea to get yourself a weekly or daily scripture to go over each morning. This doesn't ward off bad days but it does set the stage for how you will react throughout the day regardless of what happens. The bible isn't a magic potion but we can truly find reference to everything we need in it. I write down scriptures in a small journal that I carry in my purse and sometimes I put them in my phone but I read them often. Even on my good days. We need to walk with God's promises the same way we walk with our cellphones and our purses.

For you to pray: *Oh God, sweet Jesus who promises to never leave me. Lord I pray that your word stays with me for all of eternity. Even when I don't know that I remember what you've said I pray that the spirit reminds me of what I know to be true. I pray that my heart, my mind, and my soul soak up all the wisdom that you are instilling in me. Lord, this season is quite the journey and at times it seems like it's a war. Day in and day out there is some type of attack on my well-being. The Devil is working overtime to make me feel like you are not walking with me. He wants me to succumb to the obstacles that he's placed in my path. But GOD, I know that you are amazingly good. You are wonderful and your works are mighty. Your promises never return void and they are the same words that I use to fight off the Devil. Lord, I want to always be in remembrance of you. In the morning time, in the afternoon, in the evening, on my good days, and on my bad days. In Jesus name, Amen.*

Day 12 – Everything is going to Work out for Your Good

And we know that all things work together for good to those who love God, to those who are the called according to His purpose.
Romans 8:28

    I know, I know. This is what everyone says, "Don't worry, it's all going to work out". It seems like that's the go to response when something terrible is going on. As much comfort as it's intended to bring it is not the response that any of us want to hear when it seems like our world is falling apart. The promise that things will eventually work themselves out and we'll look back and smile seems like a farfetched reality that we're not privy to. It's hard to imagine a future that includes love and happiness when your past seems to be full of so much heartbreak and rejection.

    I know this feeling oh too well. Many times my friends would tell me that things would work out and I would just give them a blank stare. First off, I wasn't even interested in being friends with God for some time so they couldn't back up their comments with the bible. I also just didn't believe them. Believing them, whether I was basing it on religion or not, took faith and my faith jar was currently on empty. I couldn't see the light they promised was at the end of the tunnel. I could only see the darkness that surrounded me. One of the hardest things in the world for me to do was to step out on the faith that I barely had and believe that I could only go up from where I was. Believing wasn't a magic spell that made everything better but it did make life a little bit easier. One moment at a time and one day at a time.

    Once I started to accept what God said in the bible my hope grew. When I had really bad days I was able to hold on to a little sliver of hope and that's what helped me survive. Not only did

God promise that it would work out, he promised that it would work out for my good. One day every SINLGE thing, not some things, would benefit me. Hold on to hope, even if it's just a little bit of it. Hold on to it and don't let go. It is going to work out in your favor. One day you'll look back and be grateful that everything happened just the way it did. Even if you don't like it or you never want to relive certain moments again. You'll still be able to look back and smile because you'll know that those rough moments helped to form you into the beautiful woman that you are and will become. Just in case no one has told you, there is a light at the end of your tunnel and it is beautiful.

For you to pray: *Dear God, if I can be honest with you it is a little tough to believe that everything is going to work out. I desperately want to ask you and everyone else, when? When is it going to be my turn to have some good fortune? Nothing so far seems to have worked out for any kind of good in my life. I just don't see the nights of non-stop crying being something that's favorable for me. This is where I need you to step in God. I want to believe your word right now because I want to be able to trust you with my life but it is very hard. I know that you do have my best interest at heart. You are looking out for me even when it seems like you're not. So God, please don't give up on me as I do what I need to do in order to grow my faith in you. I want you to send me a wave of peace. The kind of peace that surpasses all understanding. I want to be able to tell myself that it will work out and I want to believe it. Amen.*

Day 13 – Chosen and Set Apart

"Before I started to put you together in your mother, I knew you. Before you were born, I set you apart as holy. I chose you to speak to the nations for Me."
Jeremiah 1:5

There are people whose love story seems to be that of a fairytale. I'm sure they have their fair share of issues but, to us looking in, their story can seem so simple. Then there are those of us going about on this single journey wondering why life and love have to be so complicated. Why couldn't we marry the first guy we fell in love with? Why did it have to lead to this road? What we don't realize is that nothing in our life comes as a surprise to God. Not only will the journey we're on be for our good but God will also use it for the good of other women just like us.

Personally, I was never interested in being chosen by God. I didn't want to be different. I wanted to just go through life doing my own thing and blending in. I did not want God to call me out of the crowd and tell me that he chose me for a different life. But he did and used my love life to make it clear. In dating the wrong guy after the wrong guy I realized that I was not supposed to just date any random man or have any kind of random relationships. God used those troubling times to let me know that I was a special kind of woman and he chose me for a special kind of man. He chose me for a different kind of life. The kind of life that would lead me here to let you know that this part of your life is not the final stop. God has so much in store for you.

It took me some time to accept this truth so I understand if it takes you a moment as well. Know that there is something wonderful about being known before you're even created. Before your parents even thought of you, God thought about you. He knew that one day the world would be graced with your presence and you would do magnificent things. He also knew that you wouldn't be excited about being single or the broken road that led you here. Most importantly, he knows what's next. So life may seem horrible and even wonderful at the same time but take heart in knowing that God chose you. He could have picked any other woman but he picked you out of the crowd and said he would use you to do great things for Him. It is a wonderful honor to be chosen by the maker of the universe.

For you to pray: *Father God, in the name of Jesus... Lord I want to thank you for choosing me. Like so many that have come before me I am honored. I know at times I can seem ungrateful and unhappy about being in this situation but please forgive me. Forgive me for not realizing that the troubling road that led me here was all a part of your plan. You know me God from the inside out. It doesn't get any better than that. Lord, while I'm in this season I pray that you teach me the things you want me to know. Teach me how to help your daughters and shine a light into their life. God, I thank you for choosing me, for setting me apart and declaring holiness over my life. Amen.*

Day 14 – How He Loves You

But God demonstrates his own love for us in this: While we were still sinners, Christ died for us
Romans 5:8

What is the greatest gift in the world that you could give to someone you love? Think about the person you love the most; the person you think loves you the most. Would you take a bullet for them? Would they take a bullet for you? I'm willing to guess that without hesitation your answer is yes. Hopefully that situation never happens but the bible tells us that there is no greater love than the love of a man who will lay down his life for his friends. That is exactly what Jesus did. He demonstrated that love for us when we were on our worst behavior so that we could live.

This is the kind of love that I want from my friends. Most importantly this is the kind of love I want from my husband. In the meantime, I would just have to learn to accept that God loved me that much and let that be enough. That used to be an extremely hard thing to do. I couldn't wrap my head around how someone who supposedly loved me so much would allow such horrible things to happen to me. I was convinced that this kind of love was not real. There was no possible way that God loved me and just let me cry myself to sleep night after night over guy after guy. Then I decided that suicide was the answer. So I tried to take my own life and in that moment (that I wasn't dying) I felt like I was witnessing God fight Satan for my life. It was the strangest thing ever but when I finally came to I realized that God had been there all along. Fighting for the life that I was ready to end because he loved me just that much. That's what we do for people we love. We fight for them.

Hopefully your realization moment isn't as traumatic. If it is the fact that you're still alive says a lot. We may have moments where we completely let go of God but he doesn't let go of us. When we are acting out and going around like we are not His children He is still there. Saving us from ourselves time and time again. He is dying for us while we sin so that we could have life and start again. He loves us just that much to do all of this over and over again if it means that we will live. This is the kind of love that we have been searching for in the men that we have cared for. As much as other people love us this kind of love can only come from God. He is the only one that can love us with a force so strong that the core of our soul is rocked. We just have to embrace that love and ride the wave with him.

For you to pray: *Dear God, how you love me. I'm so blessed to be loved by you God and to be cared for in only a way that you could care for me. There is absolutely nothing greater than the love that you pour down on me. I want to be overflowing in your love. God I want to be able to love without flaw. I want to be able to love other people so deeply that they know that type of love comes from you. Thank you Jesus for setting the example, for raising the bar when it comes to love. When I am rejecting your love because of pain remind me God of the many times you saved me. You love me so much and I just want to experience that forever from you. Amen.*

Week 3

This week is for you. During this journey it's equally important to work on yourself. If you lose everything else at the end of the day you will always have yourself. Even if, God forbid, you lose your faith you will still be left with you. A lot of times people go from person to person so often that they don't know how to be by themselves. That's extremely dangerous and it causes for a person to depend on another person as their reason for existence. That's not how God created us. He did make us to interact with one another and share our lives with them but he didn't make other people to replace who we are to ourselves. Learn to love yourself and the things that make you happy. Get yourself to a place where you can safely co-exist with another person but be 100% content with yourself.

Britt

Day 15 – Finding Yourself

Do everything in love.
1 Corinthians 16:1

What is it that you love to do? What can you do most days that make you feel happier and more content than a kid in a candy store? I think that finding yourself in the things that you love to do are an important aspect of your single journey. Whenever we put our hands to things that don't give us joy we find ourselves miserable. Of course everything we do may not make us the happiest but it should be adding some sort of benefit to our lives. When we make sacrifices for other people the idea that we're being kind should sometimes be enough to warm our hearts.

What about you? I used to ask myself that question all the time. I spent the majority of my life doing things I didn't want to just to satisfy other people, especially the men that I dated. All for us to end up not together. That's why I feel like being single is the perfect time to find yourself. It is the one season in life that is solely about you and your happiness. Of course if you have children and other people you are responsible for, they are important too. However, there is nothing quite like not having to worry about a mate. I enjoy dating and I love having a significant other in my life to make happy. However, I thoroughly enjoyed the days where I could come home and do what I wanted. I could read or write as long as I wanted because I didn't have to make plans to with someone else to help a relationship grow.

What you must understand is that if God has called you to be married then this season of singleness is temporary. It is going to end and only God knows when. So, if I could give you some really good advice then I would tell you to find out who you are. Of course you will find yourself in God but what will you be putting your hands to when you're not reading the bible. What do you enjoy doing when you're not having praise and worship? Typically the things that give you the most joy are linked to your passion and your passion is directly connected to your purpose. If you lose everything and everyone in your life you will always have yourself and God would expect you to be content with just you. Find out who that person is.

For you to pray: *Dear Heavenly Father. I'm so thankful for you making me to be the person that I am. I know that regardless if I know myself or not you have made me to be wonderful. Lord, I want to know myself and do the things that bring me joy. If I have forgotten what those things are please help me to remember. Please put the right people and the right activities in my path to help me remember what I once loved. And God, once I find myself again let me never forget her. I will always have you... But I will also always have me. I want to be able to rest easy at night knowing that I did something during the day that brought me happiness. I want to know myself so well that no one can ever make me feel less than what you have made me to be. God, I thank you for exposing me to my own self all over again. In Jesus' name. Amen.*

Day 16 – Happiness for Other People

Be happy with those who are happy. Be sad with those who are sad
Romans 12:15

Even if we live a life of contentment there will always be someone who has what we want. Someone will always be a step ahead and someone will always be a step behind us. Sometimes, when you're single, it seems like everyone around you is happy in love. You stick out like a sore thumb amongst your friends because you don't have a significant other to go out on date night with. During this time you have two choices. You can develop an attitude of joy for them or you can develop an attitude of bitterness and resentment.

I'll tell you this, it is not their fault that they are in a relationship and it certainly isn't your fault that you are single. Once upon a time I found myself being extremely bitter towards my friends who all, conveniently, happened to be in a relationship. Here I was having break-up after break-up and they were happily in love for years. I used to have parties and make them Girls Night because I didn't want anyone to bring their boyfriend. I couldn't stand to see them parade their happiness in my face. It was horribly selfish. It took years for me to finally learn what it meant to truly be happy for them. Being happy for them didn't mean that I was never going to find a significant other. It just meant that this was their season and as a friend I needed to be happy because they were happy.

Our friends just want us to be happy for them. Regardless of what is going on in our own lives they want to be able to share the joys of their life with us too. As a friend the least that we can do is to give them the gift of true happiness. It starts with us realizing that none of this is about us individually. God is writing a different story for each of us but somehow linking us all together to fulfill his ultimate purpose. When we get so wrapped up in ourselves that we can't be happy for another we take away from their joy. We are also insulting God by telling him that his great works aren't good enough for us to rejoice in because it isn't happening to us. I'll leave you with this: If all of your friends are happily in love then it means that love is in the air and it will eventually flow over to you. Just keep living, happily.

For you to pray: *Father God, I am so grateful for everything. Lord, your word says that friendship is a beautiful gift. Sometimes I don't even realize how blessed I am to be able to do life with the amazing people that you have placed in my life. Lord, I want to be an amazing friend to them. I want to truly be able to rejoice with them in all the moments they are happy about. It is not their fault that I am single and I shouldn't hold them responsible for it by not giving my happiness to them. Help me to put my own feelings aside when it comes to other people's joy. Help me to not think about what I am missing and what they have, but to be thankful for the wonderful things you are doing in all of our lives. In Jesus' name. Amen.*

Day 17 – Forgiveness is For You

And do not give the devil an opportunity [to lead you into sin by holding a grudge, or nurturing anger, or harboring resentment, or cultivating bitterness]
Ephesians 4:27

    It is easy to be upset and to hold on to the anger that another human being caused. After all, why should we do them the benefit of giving them forgiveness? They don't deserve to get off scotch-free for the havoc they have wrecked into our lives, right? That sounds good and all but not forgiving is one of the worst things we could do for ourselves. See, forgiveness is never entirely about the next person. Whether you forgive them or not they will move on with their lives. However, un-forgiveness will stop you from moving on with your life. Nothing in life deserves to have that kind of power over you.

    Growing up I was taught [and it's in the bible] that if you don't forgive others then God won't forgive you. Obviously, I need God's forgiveness because I want to get into heaven. So I would just extend my forgiveness without thinking. It was second nature. Then one day someone did something so hurtful to me that I refused to forgive them, even though I knew better. I couldn't give them the satisfaction of thinking that it was okay to treat people a certain way. So I didn't forgive them and I kept on living life. God is so faithful because for six months he knocked on the door to my heart. I didn't know it but choosing to not forgive that person was like slowly letting poison take over. I was asking God to heal my heart but every day I was drinking a vile of poison because I was holding on to a grudge.

    We can't expect God to do what he needs to do in our life if we don't do our part by letting go of the things that are making us angry. No one told me that not forgiveness would halt my spiritual growth. No one said it would give the Devil a foothold in my life and no one told me that it would block my prayers. So I'm telling you. I want you to know that not forgiving has the potential to hinder every good thing in your life. It may be hard and releasing that anger may even hurt a bit but it will be well worth it. Forgiveness shines light through a storm and it reminds you of the mightiness of God. If there is someone who has wronged you, forgive them. You don't have to ever talk to them but forgive them in your heart. If you need to, tell yourself every day that they don't matter and that this forgiveness is for you. It is to make you better.

For you to pray: *Heavenly Father, first and foremost I ask that you forgive me for my sins. I pray against any spirit that is attaching itself to my life and harboring un-forgiveness and anger. I pray that you release me from that so that you may hear my cries. Lord, I ask that you examine my heart in the deepest places. I pray that you bring to light what may be hiding in the dark. If I am not forgiving or even if I have fooled myself that I have forgiven I pray that the truth be brought to my attention. I want the poison that comes with bitterness removed from my soul. I know that I am a sinner and I want to be able to extend the same grace to others that you extend to me. I am just as undeserving as they are. I want to be a vessel that you shine your light through. I pray that, if not today, one day I can forgive as easily as I breathe. Amen.*

Day 18 – Unplug

Everyone should look at himself and see how he does his own work. Then he can be happy in what he has done. He should not compare himself with his neighbor.
Galatians 6:4

    It is difficult to escape the pull of technology. Why would we want to anyway? We are blessed to be a part of a time where technology is so advanced that it actually makes life a little easier. We are able to do more things at once and even let our presence be known in multiple places at the same time. If used correctly it can be a beautiful feature of this modern world. The dangerous part about technology is that it gives us the world of social media. Here is where we can have a look into anyone's life and expose them to bits and pieces of our own as well. It's great when we're keeping up with friends and family but it's horrible when we're comparing our lives to that of another.

    I've always known better than to compare my portion to someone else's. I thought that looking at multiple pictures of another person's relationship and family life was innocent. Typically, the people I followed were doing other positive things as well so of course I was interested. What I didn't realize was the real reason I was drawn to some of my followers. I would like to think because they were awesome speakers and writers but that just isn't the truth. Deep down inside I was only interested in following them because of the things they were posting about their love life. I was constantly feeding my spirit with relationship this and relationship that. The first problem was that it was slowly eating at me inside because I really wanted to have a family. The second problem was that I couldn't focus on the more productive areas of my life because everything I put my mind to would have something to do with finding love.

Love is great but my single season was about growing myself. I had to unplug. As much as I enjoyed the cute family photos I needed to log off. My personal brand is extremely important to me so I needed to use my internet time to look up how I could make that better. The goal of unplugging is to gain focus on what's important. We need to have a focus that can be guided fully by God and not distracted by the life of other people. Even if they are doing amazing things, unplug so you can worry about yourself. The people you see online are probably already doing the things they want to do, the things you want to do. Letting their life be a distraction to you isn't going to get your task done. It will just occupy your time so you don't do it.

For you to pray: *Heavenly Father, I thank you for the life that you have given me. Lord, I also thank you for the life that you have given other people. When other people are put in my path let their life be a source of motivation or education for me. Please allow me to recognize the things that are distracting me and remove them from my path. I'm so blessed to be a child of yours that I don't need to compare my seed to anyone else's fruit. If there is comparison in my spirit I pray that you reach inside and pull it out. I pray that you help me to survive unplugging from the social media world so that I can redirect my focus where you need it to be, in your name Jesus, Amen.*

Day 19 – The Price We Pay to Settle

Now the one who has fashioned us for this very purpose is God, who has given us the Spirit as a deposit, guaranteeing what is to come.
2 Corinthians 5:5

You settle because you do not believe, plain and simple. This is truly the reality of all situations that we settle for. Not only does God's word promise amazing things but the world promotes it to. Nowadays it is rare that we won't see a "keep going, never settle", "don't stop believing" message somewhere. As children we were most likely taught to dream big and to go for exactly what we wanted. Then adulthood happens and what we want seems to become harder to get, so we stop trying and take what we can get. We settle.

The worst thing I did in my dating life was to settle for the wrong guy. Deep down I've always known the kind of guy that God wanted me to end up with but I wasn't meeting "God's guy". I was meeting worldly men and making due. I'm not afraid to admit that I didn't want to be alone, I wanted my days to made by the sound of some guy telling me sweet nothings in my ear. Even with the nagging feeling that something just wasn't right with ALL those men, I kept seeing them. Of course the relationships ended because what God doesn't intend will never stick. I will be the first to admit it. "Hello, my name is Britt and I've settled because I don't believe".

You can be content but the moment you settle is the moment that you are in trouble. There is absolutely nothing in our life that God hasn't set aside his best for. That most definitely includes a spouse. When you go before God and seek his face praying and learning from him, you insult him when you settle for what he did not send. You are basically telling God that his best isn't worth waiting for. You're saying that mediocrity will do because mediocrity is what satisfies the need you refuse to let God fill. Settling will always cost you your satisfaction and eventually it will come back for your happiness. Sweet and beautiful daughter of God, you are worth every good thing that God has promised to you. His best is well worth the wait.

For you to pray: *Father God, words could never explain how wonderful you are for thinking of me. Forgive me God for not believing that I am worthy of your good works and the amazing things and opportunities that you have made specifically for me. For thinking less of myself when you have clearly made me in the wonderful image of you. Lord increase my patience and increase my faith. Please give me wisdom to recognize anything less than your best and strength to walk away from it. Use me as an example Lord for other women who are struggling in the belief area. Speak through me to remind them of their own worth. In your name Jesus, Amen.*

Day 20 – The Uncomfortable Places

For God has not given us a spirit of fear and timidity, but of power, love, and self-discipline.
2 Timothy 1:7

There is a drawing I've seen a billion times on the Internet that I really like about the comfort zone. It's an illustration of one circle with the word "comfort zone" in it. Then there is an arrow that goes out from the circle and lands in some random space away from the circle. Next to the arrow it says something like "where the magic happens". I think it is absolutely perfect and honest. For the most part I have learned that most of my success came from doing something that was way out of my comfort zone so I like to think it's pretty much the same for most people.

I've never had a problem dreaming big and I most certainly believe I can do whatever I put my mind to. I'm excellent at starting things but the problem comes whenever I would hit one of those unavoidable roadblocks. My roadblock always came with a choice. I could stop and turn around or I could get my hands dirty and climb over the roadblock to get to the next level. More times than not I always turned around because getting my hands dirty was way to uncomfortable and I let fear of the next level stop me.

God didn't make us to be stagnant. As long as you are working for Him there will always be a next level that He is trying to get you to. That next place is going to be so much better than the place that you're currently in but it comes at a price. You may have to pay it in late nights, early mornings, and maybe even tears. You might even feel like you're not strong enough to get to the next level because it is requiring so much of you. I can almost guarantee you that it will be one of the most uncomfortable things you go through. But God promises that it will be so worth it. Only you and God know all the areas of your life that he is trying to grow you in during this season. I'm encouraging you to stay out of your comfort zone and stretch. Do not be afraid of the next level because God is already there. He's just waiting for you to get there.

For you to pray: *Dear God, thank you so much for your grace and your mercy Lord. Thank you for being amazing and going before me and making provisions. God I pray for courage and persistence. You already know that some days are easy and other days I feel like giving up. Remind me when I forget that you know the plans you have for me. You already know what the next level will bring. So God I ask that you increase my faith in you and decrease my fear. When the path gets rough remind me that you are still there and I can lean on you for strength. Most of all Lord I pray that you make my desires burn inside of me like fire and the only extinguisher is achieving the goal. Increase my will Lord so that no matter what I will keep going. In Jesus' name Amen.*

Day 21 – Tell Your Past Goodbye

Forget the former things; do not dwell on the past.
Isaiah 43:18

    There are so many scriptures in the bible that talk about moving forward and forgetting the things of the past. However, God could not have said it any clearer than when he spoke it in Isaiah. I believe that one of the main reasons why God wants us to forget about our past is because he knows that we cannot move forward if we keep focusing on what happened yesterday. It really doesn't matter if the memories are good or bad, we don't live in those memories anymore. So although it may bring us joy to recall those memories we still must let them go too.

    If I can be honest there is not a time in my past that I would want to relive. My childhood was amazing but I definitely don't want to be a child again. Even though I've had some really amazing seasons those same seasons brought some really horrible moments. I used to suppress my feelings so much that I had convinced myself that I had gotten over them. I was nowhere near being over any of them because I was always haunted by what happened before. Anytime I ventured into a new season I would go into it with fear because of what happened in the past. I was so determined to not repeat my history that I ended up repeating it because that's all that I focused on.

    Constant thoughts of the past (especially the bad ones) rob us of the present and the future. Our past is meant to teach us and encourage us. If there is a really bad moment then learn the lesson from it so you know how to handle the problem in the future. If there is a really amazing moment then smile and work even harder to create more amazing moments. The bible says our days are numbered so don't waste your days daydreaming and fearing something from your past. Focus on today. Yesterday is gone and tomorrow will have its own set of issues and joys.

For you to pray: *Heavenly Father, thank you for the life that you have chosen for me to live. Thank you for the good moments and the bad moments. I trust you enough to know that all of that is working for my good. Lord, there are things in my past that I wish I could do over and there are definitely things that I hope to never have to repeat. Either way God, help me to remember that the past is gone away. Thank you God for the lessons, good and bad. You have made things new in my life. If I am guilty of things I pray for your forgiveness but I also pray that I can let go of that guilt. I want to be able to enjoy the things that are happening now. The things that I am working so hard to make better. I want to live each day without fear of what will happen in the next moment. I want to enjoy today the best that I can because I'm not promised tomorrow. In your name I pray, Amen*

Week 4

The purpose of this week is to address the random things that happen on this journey while you're embracing your singleness. Of course they tie in with the first three weeks of this journey but they also stand alone. I feel like they are the little details that we don't talk about enough but somehow we randomly discover just how useful a discussion about them could be. In this week I also talked about a few things that followers of Christ don't necessarily agree with one another on. My point is not to sway you in one direction or the other but to push you closer to God so you can make the best choice for yourself. Like the other weeks, this week is also critical to your journey. I pray that you get what you need out of it.

Britt

Day 22 – Learning From Other People

Let the wise hear and increase in learning, and the one who understands obtain guidance
Proverbs 1:5

    There is a reason why we are not all in the same season. How can we expect to learn from one another if everybody is going through the same thing at the same time? God is such a brilliant God because he thought about every single person that would influence your life before you were even born. He knew that you would find friendship in younger and older people alike. Learning from people while you are single isn't always all about getting over heartbreak. Sometimes it's about things you should and shouldn't do in the future to make things a little easier for you. Sometimes you learn really important lessons that you never would have been exposed to had you not been single. Regardless, don't let other people's life experiences be in vain. Learn from the people around you.

    One of my most treasured lessons was waiting on God's timing. Of course the bible says to wait but God did me a favor and gave me real life examples. He used my friends to show me what happens when you wait for God to move in your dating life and what happens when you don't wait and take things into your own hands. I've always been the type of person that wanted what I wanted right when I wanted it. After seeing so many rushed relationships fail I would be a fool to rush my next relationship. God was exposing me to person after person who didn't wait for him and the consequences that followed. Thankfully, I had friends that showed me the benefits of waiting as well. The best part about this was that I didn't have to go through it myself to learn a lesson. God used someone else to teach me the lesson. It was up to me to choose His way or my way.

Sometimes we look at other people and we think to ourselves that their situation could never happen to us. That's so far from the truth because even if we make "God's" decisions the bad stuff we're seeing could still happen to us. In relationships we will sometimes be the teacher and other times we will be the student. Whether it's a lesson that inspires you to advance your career or it's a lesson that teachers you how not to talk to your future husband, ask yourself if you are learning the lessons you are being taught. When God is trying to teach you something you will learn it one way or another. So maximize on the opportunities when he uses other people.

For you to pray: *Father God, I thank you in advance for the lessons that you use someone else to teach me. I thank you for the hardships that I didn't have to experience just to learn. Lord, let me not miss any lesson from you. Whether you are using me or you're using someone else's situation let me recognize it and learn. I want to be wise God. I want you to guide my next steps so I am on the right path and so that I stay on the right path. I want to be able to look through my spirit notebook on the things you have taught me when I feel like I am losing my way. Teach me how to have an open heart and an open mind to be able to receive guidance from other people. I want to grow Lord. I want to get to the places you are trying to take me so use me and anyone else that you need to in order to get me there. Amen.*

Day 23 – Perspective

Enjoy prosperity while you can, but when hard times strike, realize that both come from God. Remember that nothing is certain in this life.
Ecclesiastes 7:14

    If I know one thing for sure, I know that the days of any journey have the potential to take you by surprise. Being single is a unique journey because it is where you learn how to do life by yourself. Even if you are surrounded by friends and family it is most certainly not the same as having that romantic connection with another person. I can tell you now some days will simply be easier than others and that is okay. God has designed your days so he is well aware of the ups and downs that may come with the different seasons.

    I fooled myself into thinking that I was supposed to happy all the time. Eventually I got to the point where I was completely content with being single so anytime I felt a little sad about it I would feel really bad. I had convinced myself that if I was feeling sad then I wasn't truly happy. After much prayer, bible reading, and counseling sessions I realized that no one is happy 100% of the time about anything. It's just not realistic. I want you to understand that sadness does not equal discontentment. It's an emotion that God gave us that is triggered by what's going on around us. Of course you don't want to have a full blown pity party because you're not getting what you want in life however it is okay to acknowledge that you're feeling some kind of way and then take the necessary steps to feel better.

    Without the bad days we wouldn't be able to appreciate the good days and without the good days we wouldn't even recognize the bad days. It's important to have balance in life and

God had this in mind when he designed our days because he knew that nothing would be perfect. It's not about Him being a mean God or anything like that but more about us flipping our perspective. We can either choose to bask in our sorrows and live a "woe is me" life every time we're sad or we can do the complete opposite and find the joy in the situation. Every time you find yourself feeling down I encourage you to remember that God created this day and He knows exactly what is going on in your life. If you trust God then you can trust that he will use every good moment and every bad moment to fulfill his purpose in your life.

For you to pray: *Father God in the name of Jesus, help me to trust you more. When my days are good I am the happiest and I feel my best. Although my bad days may come as a surprise to me I know that they are not a surprise to you. Lord, I rebuke Satan for trying to plant seeds of guilt in my sprit when I feel sad or hurt. Every emotion that I feel was made by you and it is my job to learn how to control my emotions and not let them overtake me. So although I may feel joy and out of nowhere see something that causes pain, I will keep my faith in you and in myself. Each emotion is just a stepping stone. I've come so far on my journey and one sad moment doesn't have the power to send me back to the bitter and brokenhearted girl I once was. God, I thank you for changing my heart, Amen.*

Day 24 – Tell Someone What You're Thinking

I stayed quiet, not even saying anything good. And my sorrow grew worse.
Psalm 39:2

There are a lot of people, good Christian people, who are against counseling. Some oppose it because they don't want to talk to other people, others simply think it's a waste of time. Whatever the reason may be I personally believe it's a subject everyone should approach with an open mind. The goal of counseling is typically to advise a better route for a situation. If you really think about it you have probably had some type of counseling session in your life whether it be with a professional or a friend. Anytime we talk to another person about our thoughts and they offer advice we are receiving some type of counsel.

I was not a fan of talking to anyone about my thoughts. Not even my closest friends. Even after going to counseling for over a year I still dreaded it. I was always afraid that no one would really understand how I was feeling, people really didn't care, and I also didn't want to be a burden because I knew everyone had their own problems. I had to get over that. I ended up having a serious meltdown because I couldn't keep it bottled in anymore. I learned the hard way that my friends are there so that I could talk to them. I really needed professional help as well and there was no need for me to feel crazy about getting it. God gave each of us gifts and he gave therapists a special dose of patience and problem solving skills so that they could help people like me get to a better place.

If you are hesitant about opening up to people about your thoughts you need to get out of your head. If you trust your friends enough to call them friends then trust that they truly want to hear about your joys AND sorrows. People are not mind readers and you can't expect them to know what you are thinking because you act a certain way. I get that you might not know who to trust so I would advise you to pray about that. All of my friends are wonderful but I've learned who I can talk to what about and that's so important to know. Even with great intentions the wrong person can steer you the opposite way that God is trying to take you. The same goes for professional help. Pray about God's guidance too. I promise you that if you just allowed other people to be there for you the load you're carrying will seem a lot lighter.

For you to pray: *Heavenly Father, I thank you for my life and the people you have created to be in it. I know that no one could ever replace you and the guidance you give me but God open my heart to letting other people in. Help me to seek out the right people to talk to. Lord use them to help guide me to the place where you are trying to get me to. Keeping things in and smiling when I'm sad is tiresome. I want to be able to just be myself with people and I want to do it without fear of rejection. Lord, if I have the wrong people in my life for this task please remove them so that I can have room in my life for the right people. God I also pray that you give me a listening ear and a welcoming spirit so that my friends can feel comfortable enough to talk to me as well. In your name Jesus I pray, Amen.*

Day 25 – Dating

He who finds a wife finds a good thing, and gets favor from the Lord.
Proverbs 18:22

There are so many different opinions about whether a person should date or whether they shouldn't. I will start by saying what you decide to do is entirely up to you and God. By no means should your decision be based off of what another person says is wrong or right. It's no secret that I am an advocate for dating. I think it can be fun and exciting if it's done properly. However, I am thoroughly exhausted from it. I am definitely ready to meet and just be with the person God designed for me and I'm completely content with being single and not going on another date until he comes. But this is me and what works for my life.

Whether you want to go out on dates or not what you should not be doing is looking for a husband. It just does not work that way. As women, we go wrong when we date guys and start wondering to ourselves if this guy or that guy is the right guy for us. Dating should be fun and that kind of wondering takes the fun out of it. It also sets you up for heartbreak when that guy turns out to not be the one. Trust me. I've been there and it's not a good feeling. I used to think every single guy I dated was going to be my husband. Every guy. Now that I'm no longer with any of them I realize why they could never be my husband and I'm also very grateful to God for not choosing them for me. However, because I was convinced they were going to be mine forever I gave more of myself than I should have. I also missed all the signs that told me just how awful they were for me.

Relief came when I finally decided to stop doing that and just let God be God. It was so much easier to get to know the next guy

I met because the last thing on my mind was whether I was going to marry him or not. Just taking things one day at a time and letting a person determine who they will be in your life is one of the most stress free things ever. Trust God Lovely, whether you choose to date or not just trust God. He knows that you desire a husband and he is going to let that man find you at the right time. You don't have to search for him or even wonder about it. I firmly believe that when it is the right guy God will reveal it to you. So just breathe and have fun.

For you to pray: *Heavenly Father, Lord I thank you for the wisdom and guidance you have given me so far. I pray for you to continue guiding me when it comes to dating. I don't want to do anything outside of your will and I definitely don't want to entertain anyone that you do not have for me. Whether they are a friend or a romantic interest I pray for discernment when letting new people in my life. Lord, I also pray for patience. I pray that I will be able to wait for the right man from you to find me. I pray that when I do meet him your Holy Spirit guides me to know it. Whether I date or not Lord, I leave my love life in your hands. I am following your direction because I know that you already have the ending written. Amen.*

Day 26 – Don't Compromise Your Convictions

I have placed the Lord always in front of me. Because He is at my right hand, I will not be moved.
Psalm 16:8

    A great thing about the single journey is that you have the opportunity to figure out what you like and what you don't like. You also have the opportunity to think about the things you will and will not put up with in your next relationship and what boundaries you may set. Thinking about these things are important but not nearly as important as actually acting them out. You will meet a man. I don't know if he will be the right guy but I'm almost 100% sure that at some time during your single season you will meet a new guy and you need to be so firm in your decisions that your spirit convicts you the moment you even think about swaying.

    Do not fold. Whatever it is, whoever it is, do not let anything influence your decision to change your mind about what you know you really want to do in your heart. This can be hard because relationships are all about compromising. However, if you know that you are not going to put up with a man treating you with anything less than respect then you need to stand firm in that decision if he acts up. I used to make a ton of decisions and the moment I met a nice guy all those things went out the window. I was more afraid to lose the company of this man so I never stood up for what I believed in or wanted. I just went along with the flow. Don't do that. Do not go along with any flow unless it's something you are really okay with.

    I'm not saying that all men are bad but the reality is that there are some men out there that will try and pull you into their direction if they don't like yours. I want to encourage you to take your thoughts to God and ask him to give you strength to stand firm in your decisions. Any man that is willing to compromise your beliefs for his happiness is not the right person for you. Knowing this takes trust in God. You want to get to a place where you trust God so much that you don't sway or compromise on the wrong topic. No man is worth you feeling like you're giving up a piece of your soul to keep him. The wrong man isn't going to stay anyway. So yes, sweet and beautiful daughter of God, have the conversation with God about what you will and will not put up with. Then when the opportunity presents itself do not put up with anything less than what is in your heart.

For you to pray: *Father God, I draw near to you in my moments of weakness. I know that compromising my peace and going against what it's in my heart will only bring temporary satisfaction. That's not what I want for myself and I know that's not what you want for me either. My past relationships have taught me a lot and I know that if I want my next one to be different then I need to behave differently. Lord, give me the strength to stand up for what I believe in. Let my courage be so firmly rooted in you that I will not sway in my mind. Help me to remember that compromising will not get me what I want, especially if you say it is not meant to be. Also God, please give me the wisdom to know the difference between the things I should compromise on and the things I should not. I know that nothing is perfect but that doesn't mean I get to be unhappy. Keep me close to you God so I don't unnecessarily cause pain to myself. Amen.*

Day 27 – Male Friends

The righteous choose their friends carefully, but the way of the wicked leads them astray.
Proverbs 12:26

    Whether or not a person should have friends of the opposite sex creates just as much of a debate as dating. Everyone has an opinion about what other people should do in their lives. I don't disagree or agree with anyone's choice. I am just an advocate for people doing what God leads them to do. Regardless if you choose to be friends with men or not you should be picking your friends wisely. If you are going to have male friendships then it's wise to set up boundaries. It's also recommended to be on the same page with that person. Meaning one person cannot be romantically interested in the other person. If you're going to be friends with a guy you want it to be a pure friendship. You also want that person to be a positive influence in your life and push you the right way.

    I know a lot of men but I don't consider very many of them actual friends. I'm still on good terms with a few of the guys that I dated and although we may catch up every now and again I still wouldn't call them *friend*. I'm also very careful about my interactions with men who I know have feelings for me that I don't share. I do have a few really good male friends. These are men that I know are pure in heart and are truly not trying to lead me the wrong way. They respect me and they respect my relationships with other people. These are men that I don't have to worry about making advances towards me if I'm having a weak moment, instead they steer me towards better choices. These are people who have truly taken the time to get to know me as a person and what makes me who I am and they remind me of just how great and deserving of good things I am.

If you are open to having friends of the opposite sex then pray hard about it. The last thing you want is to be putting your trust in a man who is only pretending to be a friend but is secretly trying to get you in bed. More importantly pray for self-control. Don't pervert a good friendship because you are lonely and they are a good guy. Just because they are a good guy doesn't mean they are the guy for you and if they are let God do his work. I personally don't discriminate against anyone the Lord is trying to use in my life. There are so many examples of beautiful man/woman friendships and there are probably just as many examples of man/woman friendships gone wrong. Let God be the one to tell you who is for you!

For you to pray: *Father God in the name of Jesus, I pray that you tell me what to do when it comes to my friendships. I live in a world where your followers are either for it or against it but God I want to do what you want me to do and not what everyone else thinks I should do. If there is a man that exist who you want me to continue being friends with or become friends with in the future then I'm okay with that because I know it's your doing. If true friendship with a man isn't what you have for my life then I'm absolutely okay with that too, my girlfriends are more than enough. Lord, I just don't want to stand in your way and block out my blessings. I want to be wise in picking friends but most importantly I want to be a great friend to other people. Amen.*

Day 28 – Sin Will Stop You

If we confess our sins, he is faithful and just to forgive us our sins and to cleanse us from all unrighteousness.
1 John 1:9

In the bible we can find a list of the sins that will separate us from God. None of us are perfect so at some point we all commit one of those sins. The question is: Do you continue to live in that sin or do you ask God for forgiveness and try to do better? What I want you to understand is that you do not have to let your sin make you feel like a guilty and horrible person. However, you also don't want to purposely continue doing the very thing you know you're not supposed to be doing and then ask God to bless you. God is faithful and sometimes He chooses to bless us still while we are in the midst of our sin but this doesn't give us the right to take advantage of His grace.

We all have our own set of struggles and sometimes being unmarried will increase those struggles. Especially if the majority of your single and dating life has been you doing your own thing. Let me tell you from my own experience, trying to date *holy* is one of the hardest things I've ever had to do. I can admit that sometimes I feel like the world's way is just a little more entertaining. Sometimes I even fall off the path and do the very things I'm not supposed to be doing. But you know what? I have reached a point where my relationship with God is more important than anything else. Anything that separates me from him blocks my vision and prevents me from fulfilling His purpose for me. So when I do find myself sinning, whether I did it on purpose or not, I just ask God for forgiveness and help.

God doesn't want us to be separated from him but he will give us free will to choose. If you truly want to glorify God on your single journey then ask him to help you. I am a living witness that he will remove any and all desires from you that are not of him. You just have to ask. At the end of the day sin is going to be the one thing that will keep us from inheriting the kingdom of God. Although we are not perfect, God has sent someone who is to save us from our sins. We just have to reach up and grab his hand. Don't miss your purpose because your sin is blocking your view.

For you to pray: *Oh God, I call upon you on this day to save me. Lord please forgive me of my sins. The ones that I know of and the ones that I'm unaware of. Lord if I am committing a sin and I do not know please bring it to my attention so that I won't be blindly walking away from you. I know God that I will never be perfect but with your help I can live a life that is pleasing to you. God, help me to not feel so guilty about my sins that I don't seek your face and ask for forgiveness. You have seen me at my worst and proved time and time again that you can save me from myself. God I want to feel your presence in my life and I want to be able to walk in your will. I don't want to be affiliated with anything that will block me from you. Lord I ask that you reach deep down inside of me and pull out anything that is not of you. Renew my entire being and make me whole again. Thank you Jesus. Amen.*

Week 5

The next 2 days are to wrap up this entire journey. You are so amazing for continuing this journey with me. Know that I have included you in my prayers. I pray that God will use these devotionals in your life and that he also uses you to help someone else. I know for sure that God will come through to meet every desire of your heart in bigger and better ways than you could ever imagine. I just pray that you will wait... It will so be worth it.

All my love,
Britt Dion

Day 29 – Your Journey is Unique

Every one of us will give an answer to God about himself.
Romans 14:12

There are no two people in the world that are exactly the same. It would be kind of difficult for us to all be wonderfully made and be the same. There isn't anything wonderful about being just like another person. Since we are not all made the same then we shouldn't expect for our journey to be just like another persons. It may be similar but I guarantee you it will not be exactly the same. Everything that works for one person isn't going to work for you. It's okay to take advice and guidance on how you should and shouldn't do things but do not be disappointed when your results don't line up exactly with theirs.

When I first started my single journey I was so desperate to get to the next season that I read a ton of other people's stories and then started doing all the things they said worked for them. They said not to focus on meeting a man and then I would meet him. So I stopped, or at least told myself I stopped, but no man came. One of my friends complained about not having a man and met a guy the following week. So I complained too. Clearly, if it worked for her then it must work for me too. Still no man came. Finally, some sweet soul told me that I could not look at other people's story and expect for mine to play out the same exact way. The best advice I ever got was to just wait on God and do what he told me to do.

If you must do something that someone else is doing then choose to wait on God. Even in waiting know that your results will be different. Your love story is unique to you. The only thing that is going to work for you is what God says will work for you. Our differences are what link us together or separate us and you don't grow by copying another person. You grow by going through a season that has challenges that are unique to you as a person. Even after you meet that special guy, your love story will still be different from your favorite couple's love story. We are all trying to get to the same place, Heaven. The path taken will be different for everyone.

For you to pray: *God, I don't know why I get so worked up when things don't work out for me the way they do for other people. Forgive me for insulting your specific plan for my life. Lord, please open my heart and mind so that I can accept my differences and willingly walk the path you have chosen for me. Your word says that you alone know the plans you have for me. You never said that you would deliver me out of the wilderness the same exact way you delivered the Israelites. You just promised to deliver me. Father, I am thankful that you didn't make me like anyone else. I'm so blessed to be able to have my own story. I'm blessed that you have chosen me to stand out. Even as I seek others for guidance I pray that I don't miss yours. As long as I'm walking on your path then I am safe. I pray that I will accept my differences, in your name Jesus. Amen.*

Day 30 – Rest, God Has Not Forgotten About You

For it is not yet time for it to come true. The time is coming in a hurry, and it will come true. If you think it is slow in coming, wait for it. For it will happen for sure, and it will not wait.
Habakkuk 2:3

    The 21st century is so advanced that we can get almost any and everything instant. When things don't happen when we want them to happen we look for an alternative. Instead of just waiting we assume that plan A isn't going to happen at all and we must create or find a plan B. We create disappointment by convincing ourselves that if something was going to happen then it would have happened by now. The reality is that nothing in life really works on our time. This is God's world. We are living in his time; he is not living in ours.

    It took me a very long time to let go of that thinking. I was the worst at accepting God's timing. Even during my healing process I was ready to be healed when I was ready to be healed. I didn't care what God was trying to teach me or where he was trying to take me because I was always anxious to get to the next step when I felt like I was ready. It took a lot of therapy, and I mean a lot, for me to finally accept that things will happen when God says they will happen. Whining and throwing temper tantrums isn't going to get God to move any faster in my life if he is not ready.

    Sweet and beautiful daughter of God, I want you to know that you can rest. God has not forgotten about you. He knows exactly what is going to happen in your life and he knows when. Do not take matters into your own hands because you cannot rush God. If you act before he tells you to move it will only lead to disaster. He is well aware of the desires in your heart because he is the one that planted them there. The goals you want to achieve, the husband, and maybe even the little babies will all happen at the right time. Delay is not denial. It may seem like it's taking a while but his promises for your life are coming. When they arrive you will be so thankful that they didn't come a moment sooner. God knows you better than you know yourself so he knows exactly when you will be ready to receive the blessings he has in store for you. Just wait.

For you to pray: *Heavenly father from whom all blessings flow. Lord I thank you for not giving me anything that I am not ready for. I thank you for preparing my mind so that when you bless me with my desires I will be able to handle them appropriately. God, I just pray for patience to wait on you and not complain and I also ask for strength to keep waiting when I get tired. I know your promises don't return void. Lord, forgive me for rushing you and having a fit when you don't move. You are so good to me and I am thankful that you remember me. Amen.*

I would love to hear from you. You can contact me:

By mail: PO Box 568852 Orlando, FL 32856
Email: Hello@BrittDior.com
Social Media:
Instagram: @DiorWrites
FB: www.facebook.com/diorwrites
Twitter: @DiorWrites

Visit my website www.BrittDior.com to keep up with updates from me.

CPSIA information can be obtained
at www.ICGtesting.com
Printed in the USA
FSHW021433280719
60465FS